**Accelerated Reader**

**Book Level** 2.9 **AR Pts** 0.5

**Lexile** 440

# A NOTE TO PARENTS

When your children are ready to "step into reading," giving them the right books is as crucial as giving them the right food to eat. **Step into Reading Books** present exciting stories and information reinforced with lively, colorful illustrations that make learning to read fun, satisfying, and worthwhile. They are priced so that acquiring an entire library of them is affordable. And they are beginning readers with a difference—they're written on five levels.

**Early Step into Reading Books** are designed for brand-new readers, with large type and only one or two lines of very simple text per page. **Step 1 Books** feature the same easy-to-read type as the **Early Step into Reading Books**, but with more words per page. **Step 2 Books** are both longer and slightly more difficult, while **Step 3 Books** introduce readers to paragraphs and fully developed plot lines. **Step 4 Books** offer exciting nonfiction for the increasingly independent reader.

The grade levels assigned to the five steps—preschool through kindergarten for the Early Books, preschool through grade 1 for Step 1, grades 1 through 3 for Step 2, grades 2 through 3 for Step 3, and grades 2 through 4 for Step 4—are intended only as guides. Some children move through all five steps very rapidly; others climb the steps over a period of several years. Either way, these books will help your child "step into reading" in style!

*Library of Congress Cataloging-in-Publication Data*
Mayer, Mercer.
Purple pickle juice / written by Erica Farber and J. R. Sansevere.
  p.  cm. — (Mercer Mayer's critters of the night)  (Step into reading. A step 2 book)
SUMMARY: Thistle Howl desperately wants to grow, but drinking purple pickle juice doesn't help
and her aunt's magic makes Thistle think that maybe she's content just as she is.
ISBN 0-679-87366-X (trade) — 0-679-97366-4 (lib. bdg.)
[1. Growth—Fiction.  2. Self-acceptance—Fiction.  3. Magic—Fiction.]
I. Farber, Erica.  II. Sansevere, John R.  III. Title.  IV. Series: Mayer, Mercer. Critters of the night.
V. Series: Step into reading. Step 2 book.
PZ7.M462Pu  1996
[E]—dc20  94-43913

Printed in the United States of America    10  9  8  7  6  5  4  3  2  1
STEP INTO READING is a trademark of Random House, Inc.

 A BIG TUNA TRADING COMPANY, LLC/J. R. SANSEVERE BOOK

Step into Reading™

# MERCER MAYER'S

# CRITTERS OF THE NIGHT™

# PURPLE PICKLE JUICE

A Step 2 Book

Written by
Erica Farber and J. R. Sansevere

Random House New York

Wanda  Jack  Thistle  Axel

Capt. Short Bob  Dracul Duck  Wolf Mous

Groad        Frankengator        Moose Mummy

Uncle Mole        Zombie Mombie        Auntie Bell

This is Thistle Howl.

This is Old Howl Hall.

Thistle Howl lived in Old Howl Hall.

Thistle had a brother named Axel.

She had a mother named Wanda.

And she had a father named Jack.

As you can see, Thistle Howl

was the smallest Howl of all.

Every morning, Thistle Howl
ate a big breakfast
and drank a big glass
of purple pickle juice.

She drank a big glass
of purple pickle juice
because she thought
that purple pickle juice
would make her grow.

When she finished
her purple pickle juice,
Thistle Howl marched upstairs
to her bedroom.
And she closed her door.

Then she held her hands

high above her head

and stood on her tippy-toes and said:

    "Hands above,

      feet below.

      Grow, I say.

      Grow! Grow! Grow!"

But no matter how many glasses
of purple pickle juice she drank,
Thistle Howl did not grow.
She did not grow at all.
One day, Thistle started getting mad.
She began to shout:

"Hands above,

feet below.

Grow, I say.

Grow! Grow! Grow!"

Suddenly, there was a big bang,
and a cloud of smoke filled the room.
"Thistle Howl!" called a deep voice.
It was Thistle's Auntie Bell.

"Hello, Auntie Bell," called Thistle.

"What are you doing?"
asked Auntie Bell.

"I'm making a spell," said Thistle.

"I want to grow."

"You say you want some snow?"
said Auntie Bell.
"That's easy."
Before Thistle could say a word,
Auntie Bell snapped her fingers,
rubbed her nose, and took off her shoes.
Auntie Bell took off her shoes
because her feet always swelled
when she did her magic spells.
Suddenly, it began to snow.

There was snow everywhere.

"I don't want <u>snow</u>!" said Thistle.

"I want to <u>grow</u>!"

"Row, you say?" said Auntie Bell.

"That's easy."

Before Thistle could stop her,

Auntie Bell blinked her eyes three times

and said:

> "Bubble, bubble,
>
> blueberry jam.
>
> Row, row, row
>
> as fast as you can."

As you may be able to tell,

Auntie Bell did not hear very well.

In a twinkle, Thistle and Auntie Bell
were in a boat.

"Row, row, row," said Auntie Bell.

"No! No! No!" said Thistle.

"I don't want to <u>row</u>!

I want to <u>grow</u>!"

"Grow?" said Auntie Bell.

"All you want to do is grow?

Why didn't you say so?"

"I <u>did</u> say so!" said Thistle.

"I said I wanted to grow."

"Then grow you shall," said Auntie Bell.

Auntie Bell and Thistle

flew through the woods

to Auntie Bell's little house.

"Now we are going to make
a magic potion," said Auntie Bell.
"It will make you grow!"
Auntie Bell lit a fire
under her big black pot.

Then she opened her book
of magic spells.
"This is what we need,"
said Auntie Bell.

"One bat tooth,

two frog toes,

three leaves of poison ivy,

and four cat hairs."

Auntie Bell put everything
into her big black pot.
She mixed the potion with a big spoon.
She said this big spell three times:

"Leaves of ivy, tooth of bat, toes of frog, hairs of cat. Abracadabra, strawberry pie, make Thistle grow high as the sky!"

Then Auntie Bell gave Thistle
a cup of the magic potion.

"Drink this," she said to Thistle.

"It will make you grow."

So Thistle drank the magic potion . . .

. . . and started to grow!

And grow . . .

. . . and grow!

"Auntie Bell, now I am <u>too</u> big,"
said Thistle in a big voice.
"Please make me small!"

"Small!" said Auntie Bell.

"Well, that's another spell."

Auntie Bell opened her book

of magic spells.

She threw some magic powder

up in the air.

Then she said this small spell:

"Smaller than the smallest bug,

with powder from my magic jug,

you shall be small, yes, small you'll be,

and all before you count to three!"

"One," said Thistle.

"Two," said Thistle.

Suddenly, Thistle started to shrink.

And she kept on shrinking

and shrinking

and shrinking . . .

"Now I am <u>too</u> small,"

said Thistle to Auntie Bell.

"Can't you do another spell?"

"There are no more spells,"
said Auntie Bell.
"The rest is up to you.
Now click your heels
and clap your hands and say,
'Thistle is who I am, I am.
Thistle is who I am.'"

Thistle clicked her heels
and clapped her hands.
Then she said,
"Thistle is who I am, I am.
Thistle is who I am!"
Suddenly, Thistle began to grow.

She kept right on growing

until she was her very own size.

"I don't want to be big

and I don't want to be small,"

said Thistle.

Auntie Bell just smiled.

She had known that all along.

The next morning, Thistle Howl

drank a big glass

of purple pickle juice for breakfast.

She drank a big glass

of purple pickle juice just because . . .

she liked it!